The Black Sox Scandal of 1919

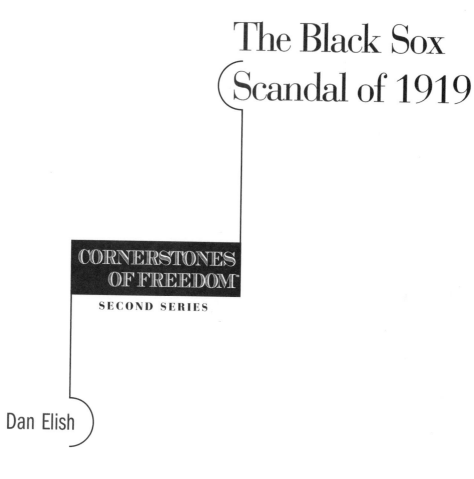

CORNERSTONES OF FREEDOM™

SECOND SERIES

Dan Elish

Children's Press®
A Division of Scholastic Inc.
New York • Toronto • London • Auckland • Sydney
Mexico City • New Delhi • Hong Kong
Danbury, Connecticut

Photographs © 2007: AP/Wide World Photos: 16; Brown Brothers: 5, 7, 11, 15 top, 18; Chicago Historical Society: 33 (Chicago Daily News, DN-0072334), 30 (Chicago Daily News, SDN-058463A), 22 (Chicago Daily News, SDN-061904), 15 third from bottom (Chicago Daily News, SDN-062958), 10 (ICHi-19569), 15 fourth from bottom (ICHi-20727), 24 (SDN-061914), 26 (SDN-063126); Corbis Images: 41 (Shaun Best/Reuters), 15 third from top, 15 second from top, 19, 25, 31, 32, 34 (Bettmann), 15 second from bottom, 15 bottom, 29 (Underwood & Underwood), 28 (UPI), 20; Getty Images: cover top (APA/Hulton Archive), 40 (John G. Mabanglo/AFP), 3 (MLB Photos), 8, 39, 21 (National Baseball Hall of Fame/MLB Photos); Library of Congress: cover bottom, 4, 12, 14, 15 fourth from top, 36; National Baseball Hall of Fame and Museum Library, Cooperstown, N.Y.: 6.

Map by XNR Productions, Inc.

Library of Congress Cataloging-in-Publication Data
Elish, Dan.
  The Black Sox scandal of 1919 / Dan Elish.
      p. cm. — (Cornerstones of Freedom)
  Includes bibliographical references and index.
  ISBN-10: 0-516-23631-8
  ISBN-13: 978-0-516-23631-5
  1. Chicago White Sox (Baseball team)—History—Juvenile literature. 2. Baseball—Corrupt practices—United States—History—Juvenile literature. 3. Baseball—Betting—United States—History—Juvenile literature. 4. World Series (Baseball) (1919)—Juvenile literature. I. Title. II. Series.
  GV875.C58E45 2006
  796.357'64'0977311—dc22   2005007525

IT WAS OCTOBER 1, 1919. EDDIE Cicotte took the mound to pitch the first game of the World Series. The ballpark was sold out. Extra tickets were being sold for as much as $50. That was an enormous amount of money in those days. Across America, fans waited for news of the big game to reach them by **telegraph**. Cicotte's team, the Chicago White Sox, was favored to beat the opposing Cincinnati Reds.

Eddie Cicotte was the starting pitcher for the first game of the 1919 World Series. At the time, he was one of baseball's best pitchers.

Cicotte threw a few warm-up pitches to his catcher, Ray Schalk. Soon Cincinnati's first batter, Maurice Rath, stepped up to the plate. Behind the plate, Schalk signaled for a fastball. Cicotte let his first pitch fly. The umpire called, "Strike!" Schalk threw the ball back to Cicotte and called for the next pitch: a curveball.

Eddie Cicotte was one of the best pitchers in baseball. That year, he had won an incredible twenty-nine games. But when Cicotte wound up and threw the next pitch, the ball curved sharply. It hit Rath in the back.

Many baseball fans were surprised. What they didn't know was that this wasn't a bad throw or a mistake. Eddie Cicotte meant to do this. The bad pitch was actually a signal he was sending to a group of gamblers, people who make a living by betting on sports or in casinos. These gamblers had paid several players on the White Sox team to throw, or lose, the World Series on

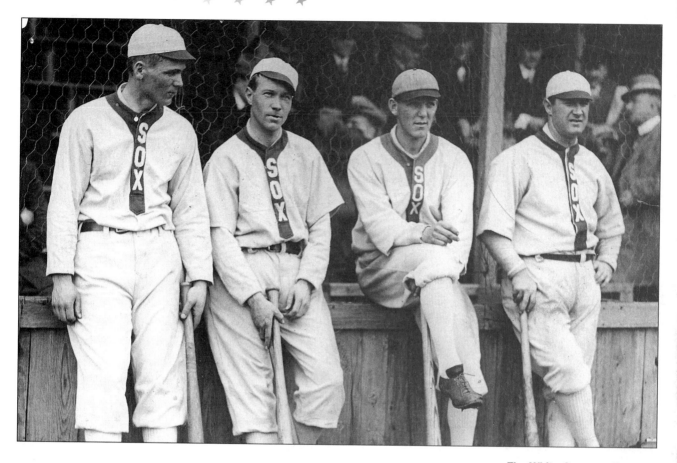

purpose. That way, the gamblers could place large bets on the less-favored Cincinnati team and make a fortune. Eddie Cicotte's bad pitch was the final signal to the gamblers: the fix was on.

The White Sox won the World Series twice in their first 104 years as an organization—in 1906 vs. the Chicago Cubs and in 1917 vs. the New York Giants. They didn't win it again until 2005.

GAMBLERS AND BASEBALL

Most fans were shocked when they learned that members of the White Sox had been charged with taking money to throw the World Series. They found it hard to believe that baseball players would cheat. In truth, there had been dishonest ballplayers since the early days of the sport.

The Cincinnati Red Stockings were the first all-professional baseball team.

Professional baseball began in 1869, when the Cincinnati Red Stockings team was founded. In 1876, the National League was organized. Players were paid salaries, and fans were charged admission to see teams play. That's also when professional gamblers saw how they could get rich. Some players accepted **bribes** to lose games on purpose. In 1877, the club from Louisville seemed to be on their way to winning the league. In a final series against the team from Hartford, they played terribly and lost. An investigation followed. Four Louisville players were found guilty of accepting bribes of around $100.

In baseball's early years, players who took bribes usually weren't caught. If they were, they weren't punished. One of the great players of the early 1900s was a first baseman named Hal Chase. Chase became an expert at throwing games for gamblers. Once, Chase told a pitcher in the middle of a game, "I've got some money bet on this game, kid. There's something in it for you if you lose." The pitcher reported Chase to the team manager, Christy Mathewson. When Mathewson told the president of the National League, the president said there wasn't enough **evidence** to throw Chase out of baseball. Instead, Chase was traded to another team and continued to play.

Hal Chase, one of the great first basemen of the early 1900s, often took bribes. Many of the players who threw games were never caught.

Charles Comiskey, a brilliant baseball strategist, spent a lot of money building Comiskey Park and his Chicago White Sox team.

Most players were honest. But it seemed that the dishonest players thought they could get away with almost anything.

CHARLES "COMMY" COMISKEY

Charles Comiskey, ex-player, ex-manager, and ex-minor league executive, and cofounder of the American League, put a team in Chicago in 1900. It was called the White

Stockings, which quickly became White Sox. In 1910, he built Comiskey Park, one of the best ballparks in the country. Now all Comiskey needed was the best team.

In 1915, Comiskey began to buy up the best talent in the league. He paid the Philadelphia Athletics $65,000 for Eddie Collins, a great second baseman. He paid another $65,000 for one of the best hitters in history: "Shoeless" Joe Jackson. He bought center fielder Oscar "Happy" Felsch from Milwaukee, a minor league team, for $12,000.

In 1917, Comiskey's team of stars won the World Series. But despite their winning record, the White Sox players were unhappy. Comiskey was a brilliant baseball **strategist**, which means he was skilled at planning how to win baseball games. But some say he treated his players badly by not paying them enough. The salaries of Comiskey's players, however, were about the same as the salaries of players on other teams.

In those days, baseball players had no union to help them get higher salaries. In fact, it was common for an owner to put what was known as a reserve clause in players' contracts. This clause said that the team had complete rights to a player's services. If the player didn't like the salary he was offered, he was not allowed to go to another team. His only option was to take what was offered or quit baseball entirely.

BASEBALL'S BEGINNING

For years, a story existed that a man named Abner Doubleday first wrote the rules for baseball in 1839 near Cooperstown, New York. Evidence exists, however, that baseball was being played in Pittsfield, Massachusetts, as early as 1791. Still, it's impossible to know exactly where the first ball game was played. As Jeff Idelson, a spokesman for the Baseball Hall of Fame says, "Baseball wasn't really born anywhere."

"SHOELESS" JOE

Joe Jackson had an unusual nickname. The story goes that Jackson once had such painful blisters on his feet that he played in a game without shoes and socks. In his bare feet, he hit a triple. While Jackson stood on third, a fan yelled, "You shoeless son of a gun!" The nickname stuck.

Some players thought Comiskey was **stingy** with more than salaries. Other teams gave their players an allowance of at least $4 to spend on meals while they were on the road. Comiskey gave his players $3. In 1917, Comiskey promised his players a bonus if they won the **pennant**, or league championship. The players assumed that this meant more money. Instead, when they won, players claimed that Comiskey gave them a case of bad champagne.

The White Sox nickname, Black Sox, may have originated when Comiskey refused to give the players money to wash their uniforms. In those days, it was common for team members to wash their own uniforms or pay to have them washed. In protest, the players decided to play in the same dirty uniforms day after day. They soon called themselves the Black Sox. The protest didn't work. In the end, the players had to continue to be responsible for their clean uniforms.

Five players from the 1917 White Sox (left to right): Harry Leibold, Eddie Murphy, Eddie Collins, "Shoeless" Joe Jackson, and "Happy" Felsch.

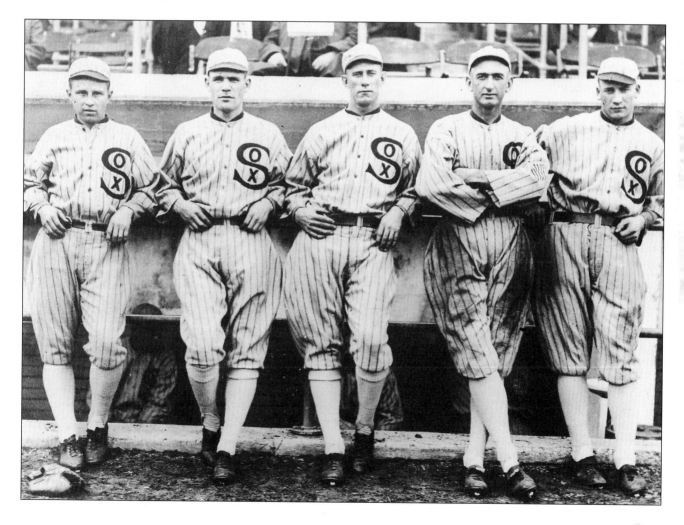

Fans piled into Comiskey Park to see the White Sox. In 1919, attendance at White Sox home games was more than six hundred thousand.

But Comiskey was very generous with younger players by giving them bonus money when they played well. He believed this would motivate them to continue playing their best. Comiskey also showed generosity to the reporters who wrote about him in the newspapers. He set up a room in Comiskey Park where reporters were given free food and drinks before each game.

* * * *

In 1919, the White Sox tore up the league, winning game after game. But Comiskey would not pay the players extra for doing what he had hired them to do: win. Finally, first baseman Chick Gandil, a good player nearing the end of his career, decided he had one final chance to make some big money before he retired. The World Series was his chance.

EIGHT MEN COME ABOARD

Three weeks before the World Series, the White Sox were playing several games against the Red Sox in Boston. Between games, on September 10, a tall man wearing a white suit and a bow tie stepped into the lobby of the Hotel Buckminster. The man was Joseph "Sport" Sullivan, a well-known gambler. Soon he was invited up to Chick Gandil's room.

In the past, Gandil had given Sullivan inside information about his team that the gambler used to make bets. If Gandil told him that a pitcher was tired, then Sullivan would bet on the other team. But this time, Gandil had something big on his mind. He told Sullivan that for $80,000, the White Sox would lose the World Series.

Sullivan was interested. This was a chance to make a lot of money. While Sullivan went off to find partners to help him bankroll $80,000, Gandil got to work on his teammates. Gandil knew that he would need to convince a sizable group of the best players to come on board to guarantee that the White Sox would lose. Most of all, he would need the team's best pitchers to agree to the fix. After all, if the pitchers let the Cincinnati players get too many hits, there was no way that Chicago could win.

UNFRIENDLY TEAMMATES

The 1919 White Sox proved that all the members of a team don't necessarily have to get along to win. Chick Gandil hated second baseman Eddie Collins so much that he didn't talk to him—not even once— all season.

Chick Gandil often gave inside information about his team to gamblers. He was the ring-leader of the Black Sox scandal.

The obvious first choice was the best pitcher on the team, Eddie Cicotte. Like many players on the team, Cicotte thought he was underpaid. Worse, some claim that two years earlier, in 1917, Charles Comiskey promised him a bonus of $10,000 if he won thirty games. When Cicotte won twenty-nine games, Comiskey ordered him benched for his last start of the season because he didn't want to pay the bonus. This story is not considered completely true. It is known, however, that Cicotte had just bought an expensive farm and was nearing the end of his career. He needed money, which may be the real reason Gandil approached him.

Still, Cicotte said no—again and again. Frustrated, Gandil almost gave up on the whole plan—until one night Cicotte sat down next to him on a train and whispered, "I'll do it for $10,000. Cash. Before the Series begins."

With Cicotte now willing, Gandil rounded up the rest. Shortstop "Swede" Risberg said yes right away. A substitute infielder, Fred McMullin, overheard Gandil and Risberg and insisted that he be in on the fix, too. Then Gandil convinced the team's second-best pitcher, Claude "Lefty" Williams, by telling him that Cicotte had already agreed to the plan. Gandil then asked the three best hitters on the team—George "Buck" Weaver, "Shoeless" Joe Jackson, and Oscar

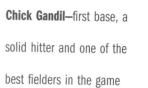

THE EIGHT MEN

Eddie Cicotte—pitcher, won twenty-nine games in 1919

Oscar "Happy" Felsch—center field, one of the best outfielders in baseball

Chick Gandil—first base, a solid hitter and one of the best fielders in the game

"Shoeless" Joe Jackson—left field, one of the best hitters in baseball history

Fred McMullin—substitute infielder, didn't play often, but was a good baseball strategist

"Swede" Risberg—shortstop, had a great throwing arm

George "Buck" Weaver—third base, one of the best players in the league

Claude "Lefty" Williams—pitcher, won twenty-three games in 1919

"Swede" Risberg was friends with Chick Gandil and acted as his main accomplice.

"Happy" Felsch—to come to a meeting in his hotel room on September 21.

At the meeting, Gandil made it clear that the eight players would receive a lump sum of $80,000 before the World Series began, to be divided equally. Looking back, it seems strange that the players would agree to such a plan. Most of them were young, with about ten years left in their careers. On the other hand, all eight players knew of baseball games that hadn't been played honestly. Most important, the men seemed to believe that fixing a World Series would be a good way to get some of the money they thought they deserved.

THE GAMBLERS

While Chick Gandil lined up the players, "Sport" Sullivan tried to raise $80,000. But it wasn't long before word of the fix spread, and other gamblers wanted a piece of the action. For starters, there was a retired major league pitcher named William Thomas Burns. His nickname was "Sleepy" because he used to fall asleep on the bench during ball games. After retiring from baseball, Burns had made a fortune in the oil industry. When he heard rumors that the White Sox were planning to throw the World Series, he grilled Gandil and Eddie Cicotte for all the details. Gandil said Burns could fund the fix if he wanted. But Gandil raised the price. Burns would have to come up with $100,000. There was only one gambler in America who could be certain to have that kind of money: Arnold Rothstein.

Rothstein grew up in poverty in New York City and became a gambler. His nickname was "The Big Bankroll." About a week before the World Series began, Burns and another gambler named Billy Maharg approached Rothstein at the racetrack and told him that the White Sox were willing to throw the World Series. Rothstein said he was not interested.

But Rothstein had an assistant named Abe Attell. Attell was nicknamed "The Little Champ" because he had once

Arnold Rothstein was a notorious gambler. He once bet $100,000 on a single roll of the dice.

"THE BIG BANKROLL"

A character based on Arnold Rothstein appeared in one of America's most famous novels, *The Great Gatsby*, by F. Scott Fitzgerald. The book was published in 1925. In it, the character is identified as "the man who fixed the World Series back in 1919."

been the featherweight boxing champion of the world. In 365 fights, he had lost only six times. Now Attell decided to go behind his boss's back. He contacted Burns and told him that Rothstein had changed his mind and was willing to fund the entire enterprise. Burns believed the lie. Of course, Attell had no idea how he would come up with the $100,000 to pay the players. At that point, he didn't care. All that mattered to him was that the White Sox go ahead with their plan to throw the World Series. That way, he could make a fortune by placing bets on the Reds.

To make matters more complicated, Rothstein eventually decided to fund the plan after all. But he didn't give his

* * * *

money to Attell or Burns. Rothstein was more impressed with Sullivan, the man Gandil had originally contacted. A few days before the World Series was to begin, Rothstein gave Sullivan $40,000 to distribute to the players. But Sullivan wasn't called a gambler for nothing. Instead of giving all the money to the players, he used $30,000 of the cash to place bets on the World Series. That left him with only $10,000 of the promised $80,000 to give to Gandil the night before the World Series began. Gandil was furious. But Sullivan promised him that there would be more money later. In the end, Gandil took the money and gave it all to Cicotte. Cicotte is said to have spent the night carefully sewing the bills inside his jacket.

Abe "The Little Champ" Attell was Arnold Rothstein's assistant.

THE WORLD SERIES BEGINS

By the time Eddie Cicotte took the mound in Cincinnati on that hot October day, word had leaked out that Chicago might lose on purpose. Some people didn't believe it. They said that the reason Cincinnati was suddenly favored to win the first game was because Cicotte's arm was sore.

A reporter named Hugh Fullerton of the *Chicago Herald and Examiner* was especially angry about the rumors. Fullerton expected Chicago to win. But when "Sleepy"

The Cincinnati Red Stockings became the Cincinnati Reds in 1876.

Burns told him to bet on Cincinnati, the reporter became suspicious. Worried, Fullerton met with Christy Mathewson, the great retired pitcher. Fullerton and Mathewson agreed to watch the games together. Whenever it seemed like a player on the White Sox team was making a mistake on purpose, they would make a note of it. On top of that, Fullerton sent a wire by telegraph to all the papers that ran his column: "ADVISE ALL NOT TO BET ON THIS SERIES. UGLY RUMORS AFLOAT."

Fullerton was right to be nervous. After hitting the first batter with a pitch, Cicotte let the Reds get one run in the first inning. In the second and third innings, Cicotte settled

Christy Mathewson had a long and successful career in baseball. He was elected to the National Baseball Hall of Fame in 1936.

down and retired the Cincinnati players easily. In the fourth inning, "Happy" Felsch made an incredible catch in the outfield, robbing Edd Roush of the Reds of a sure triple. Cicotte realized that he would have to lose the game on his own. It only made sense. After all, he was the one who had been paid the $10,000.

In the fourth inning, Cicotte fielded an easy ground ball. With a runner on first, his play was simple. He had to turn

Claude "Lefty" Williams lost all three of the games he pitched for the White Sox in the 1919 World Series.

and throw to second base to start a sure double play. But Cicotte hesitated, then threw the ball high. The White Sox got the out at second, but not at first. Then Cicotte allowed two singles in a row. Next, Cincinnati's pitcher hit a towering triple. The Cincinnati fans stood and cheered. In the end, the White Sox lost badly. The score was 9 to 1.

That night, Burns visited Abe Attell. Burns wanted to get $20,000 to pay the players for their victory. But "The Little Champ" wasn't in a giving mood. He lied to Burns by telling him that all his money had been bet. The players would have to wait. When Burns relayed the news to the players, they were angry. But Burns assured them that they would have their money before the second game.

Chick Gandil and Claude "Lefty" Williams met with Attell the following morning. Again, Attell said that he did not have the money. Instead, he showed them a fake telegram from Arnold Rothstein that read, "AM WIRING YOU TWENTY GRAND." Williams and the other White Sox players involved were still suspicious. Even so, Williams, one of the best pitchers in the league, walked on the mound and lost Game 2 by a score of 4 to 2.

After the game, the White Sox catcher, Ray Schalk, was so certain that Williams had lost on purpose that he tried to beat him up. White Sox manager "Kid" Gleason was so angry that he tried to strangle Gandil.

RING LARDNER

Ring Lardner was a sportswriter who became one of America's greatest short-story writers of the early twentieth century. After the White Sox lost the first two games of the World Series, he was certain that the team was losing on purpose. On the train to Chicago, he began to sing in front of the White Sox players:

> "I'm forever blowing ball games,
>
> Pretty ball games in the air,
>
> I come from Chi, I hardly try
>
> Just go to bat and fade and die."

In Cincinnati, fans packed the ballpark and climbed to the roofs of nearby buildings to witness the 1919 World Series.

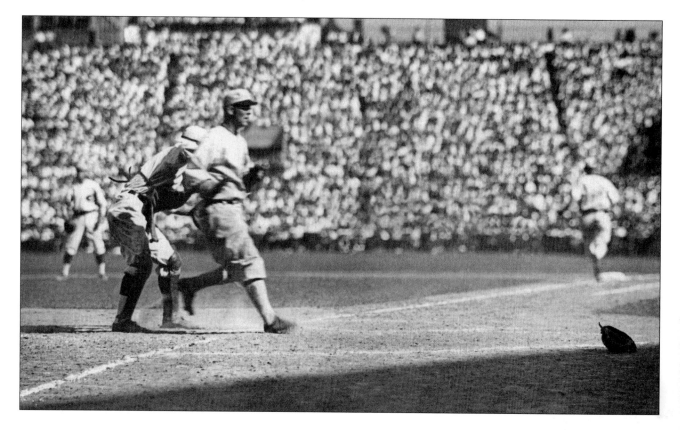

CHICAGO ROARS BACK—ALMOST

The night after the third game, Chick Gandil visited Abe Attell. Gandil demanded $40,000 for losing the first two games, but Attell came up with only $10,000. Angry, the White Sox players began to have second thoughts. Why should they keep losing if they weren't getting paid?

The next game was in Chicago. Pitcher Dickie Kerr was on the mound for the White Sox and wasn't in on the fix. Kerr pitched a great game. The White Sox won 3 to 0. Now the gamblers were angry. Many of them had bet on Cincinnati and lost.

Bill Rariden of the Cincinnati Reds tagged out "Buck" Weaver at home plate in Game 2 of the World Series. The White Sox lost the game 4 to 2.

25

Attell refused to give the players any more money. But "Sport" Sullivan returned with $20,000. Gandil divided it evenly among "Swede" Risberg, "Happy" Felsch, "Lefty" Williams, and "Shoeless" Joe Jackson. Earlier, Jackson had been promised $20,000 to participate in the scheme. Now he had to settle for $5,000. But that was more than Fred McMullin or "Buck" Weaver received. They didn't get a cent.

Today, the World Series is a best-of-seven competition. The first team to win four games wins. In 1919, the World Series was a best-of-nine competition. With some money in their pockets, the White Sox lost Games 4 and 5. Cincinnati led the Series four games to one, and they needed to win just one more game to be the world champions. White Sox manager "Kid" Gleason couldn't believe what was happen-

Dickie Kerr was the only honest starting pitcher on the White Sox team during the 1919 World Series.

ing to his team. "I don't know what's the matter," he said. "But I do know that something is wrong with my gang. . . . The bunch I have now couldn't beat a high school team."

But the gamblers had taken the players for granted too many times. Again, the players were promised more money, and again, they got nothing. On the train ride back to Cincinnati for Game 6, the players met. With no more money coming, it was time to win. For starters, the team that won the World Series received the bigger bonus. Plus, the better they played, the better chance they would have to convince Charles Comiskey to increase their salaries the following year.

The White Sox won Game 6 by one run. Weaver, Jackson, and Gandil got hits in the tenth inning. With Eddie Cicotte back on the mound and trying his best, the White Sox also won Game 7 by a score of 4 to 1. Now Chicago fans were

Claude "Lefty" Williams was told to throw Game 8 of the World Series or risk danger to his wife.

confident. Gleason told the press, "Even though we are still one game behind, we will win for sure."

But Sullivan was getting nervous. The gambler had placed all of his money on Cincinnati to win the World Series. He didn't like how well Chicago was playing. Some people believe that before the eighth game, he placed a phone call to a **gangster**. The night before the game, the gangster stopped "Lefty" Williams on the street. Williams was scheduled to take the mound the next day. The gangster told Williams that if he didn't lose the next day, something might happen to his wife. Williams was terrified. He hadn't been paid any more money, but when he took the mound on October 9, he gave up four runs in the first inning. The White Sox lost the game 10 to 5. The Cincinnati Reds were the World Series champions.

THE OFF-SEASON

The day after the World Series ended, the players finally got the big payday they had been waiting for. "Sport" Sullivan delivered $40,000 to Chick Gandil. Gandil distributed it to

Charles Comiskey entered
the off-season aware of the
rumors that his team had
thrown the World Series.

"Swede" Risberg and Fred McMullin, and kept the major share for himself. Then he went home to California to see his wife and daughter.

But Joe Jackson was feeling guilty. He went to Charles Comiskey's office, ready to confess what the players had done. For his part, Comiskey knew of the rumors. He also

Despite having received money from gamblers, Joe Jackson batted .375, an excellent average, in the 1919 World Series.

knew that they were probably true. But the last thing he wanted was for news that his team had thrown the World Series to go public. That would make him look like a fool. Also, he would have to fire some of his best players. So when Jackson appeared at his office, Comiskey refused to see him. Jackson gave up and returned home to South Carolina.

Rumors of the fix continued throughout the winter. Even though Comiskey didn't want his team investigated, he realized that he needed to do something to make it seem as though he was taking the situation seriously. He made an offer of $20,000 to anyone with information about the game fixing. Of course, most of the players and gamblers kept their mouths shut. After all, they didn't want to get in trouble. Because Comiskey really didn't want the situation investigated, he ignored the few people who did come forward with information. Again, Jackson tried to tell his side of the story. Because he had never learned to read or write, Jackson dictated a letter to his wife, confessing what had happened. When the letter arrived in Chicago, Comiskey ignored it.

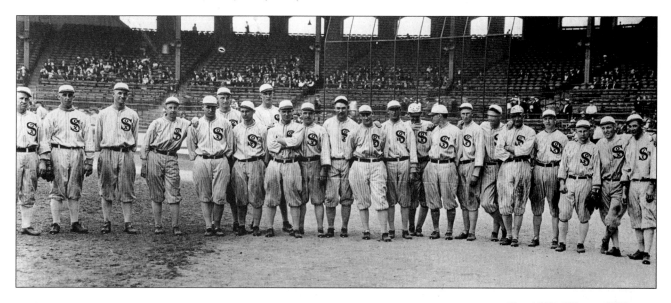

The 1920 Chicago White Sox: all eight players involved in the 1919 scandal, except Chick Gandil, returned to the team.

Comiskey was already thinking about the next season's team. Though Gandil had retired, Comiskey hoped to re-sign the rest of his players. But most of them refused to sign their contracts unless they were given more money. Reluctantly, Comiskey gave out some small raises. One by one, the players came aboard. On opening day in 1920, roughly the same team took the field.

Again, the White Sox had a good year. Eddie Cicotte and Claude "Lefty" Williams pitched as well as ever. Early in the season, Jackson was hitting an unbelievable .400. Still, talk of the 1919 World Series would not go away. Some suspected that the White Sox were still throwing games. Worse, there were rumors that players on the Giants, Yankees, Braves, Red Sox, and Indians were also working with gamblers.

By the end of August, the White Sox were in a three-way race for the pennant with the Cleveland Indians and the

A grand jury began hearings to investigate baseball gambling just weeks after Chicago newspapers complained of corruption.

New York Yankees. When the White Sox lost a three-game series to a much weaker Boston team, second baseman Eddie Collins was so suspicious about his teammates that he complained to Comiskey. Then there were widespread reports of gambling in a game between the Chicago Cubs and the Philadelphia Phillies. By then, the cheating was too obvious to ignore. Reporter Jim Crusinberry wrote an open letter to baseball. Part of it read, "It occurs to me that the game must be cleaned up at once . . . if baseball is going to survive."

In September 1920, with the public crying out for action, Illinois's state attorney Maclay Hoyne gave permission for a **grand jury** to be formed. Its initial goal was to investigate the rumors of gambling at the ball game between the Cubs and the Phillies. But the grand jury was also authorized to look into the 1919 World Series.

THE GRAND JURY AND TRIAL

For most of the 1920 season, the eight White Sox players tried to forget about the 1919 World Series. So did Charles Comiskey. In late September, his team was in the thick of the pennant race. "Shoeless" Joe Jackson was hitting an amazing .387. If the White Sox made it to the World Series again, Comiskey was determined they would play, no matter what the suspicions against them.

As it turned out, Chicago lost the pennant to Cleveland. With public pressure mounting, the White Sox players began to confess. The first to face the grand jury was Eddie Cicotte. With tears in his eyes, he said, "I don't know why I did it. . . I must have been crazy! . . . I needed the money. I had the wife and the kids." Then Cicotte explained the plan from the

Assistant State Attorney Hartley Replogle called many of baseball's famous figures to testify before the grand jury.

THE CONFESSION

During part of Eddie Cicotte's confession, he said, "I've lived a thousand years in the last twelve months. I would not have done that thing for a million dollars. Now I've lost everything, job, reputation, everything."

beginning. Later, he told the grand jury how easy it was to throw a game. "I did it by not putting a thing on the ball. . . . A baby could've hit 'em."

Meanwhile, the seven other players were getting nervous. Finally, Jackson couldn't take it anymore. He called the judge who was overseeing the grand jury and asked if he could come in and make his confession. He was cross-examined by Hartley Replogle, the assistant state attorney.

REPLOGLE: Did anybody pay you any money to help throw that Series in favor of Cincinnati?

JACKSON: They did.

REPLOGLE: How much did they pay?

"Shoeless" Joe Jackson (right) confessed to Hartley Replogle on September 28, 1920. Yet when the trial began on July 18, 1921, his confession, among others, had been lost.

JACKSON: They promised me $20,000, and paid me five.

That afternoon, on September 28, Comiskey released a telegram to the press. He suspended all eight players, saying, "If you are innocent . . . you will be **reinstated**."

Next, the grand jury called Arnold Rothstein to testify. It was rumored that Rothstein had won $270,000 in the 1919 World Series by betting on Cincinnati. Still, he denied knowing anything about the fix. He said that the whole thing had been Abe Attell's idea. Rothstein spoke of his great love of the game. He mentioned that he was a close friend of John McGraw, the manager of the New York Giants. Throughout the examination, Rothstein was treated with great respect.

In the end, the grand jury **indicted**, or charged, all eight players, along with Hal Chase. The gamblers—Attell, "Sport" Sullivan, Bill Burns, and some of Rothstein's thugs—were also indicted. The following June, the White Sox players were tried for conspiring to defraud the public and hurt the business of Charles Comiskey.

Comiskey had a lot of money tied up in his eight players. After all, he had paid $65,000 each for Cicotte and Jackson. He knew that if the players were found not guilty, they would probably be allowed to play baseball again. Mysteriously, when the case against the eight players went to trial in July 1921, the grand jury records of the confessions of Jackson, Cicotte, and Williams were missing. The jury

SAY IT AIN'T SO!

The most famous story to come out of the 1919 World Series scandal is said to have occurred when "Shoeless" Joe Jackson walked out of the courtroom. A little boy cried to him, "Say it ain't so, Joe!" Jackson looked at the boy sadly and replied, "I'm afraid it is, kid." Over the years, Jackson denied many times that this exchange took place.

Judge Landis banned all eight White Sox players from baseball for life. Many believe this action restored the public's faith in the game.

found the eight men not guilty. A "not guilty" verdict is not the same as being innocent. Members of the jury may have believed that some, or all, of the players were guilty. But without the most important evidence, the confessions, the jury didn't have enough proof of the players' guilt.

Cheers erupted from the spectators who had filled the courtroom to watch the trial. The players jumped up and shook hands with the jurors. Their attorney called the men "the most mistreated ballplayers in history." That night, the eight players celebrated at a local restaurant. It seemed that things were finally going their way. But more bad news was just around the corner.

JUDGE LANDIS

Prior to 1919, Major League Baseball was governed by a three-man commission. After the scandal of 1919, most owners believed that the sport needed a central authority with more power. The owners disbanded the three-man commission. In its place, they created the position of a single, powerful baseball commissioner. This man would have extraordinary authority to run baseball the way he saw fit.

The man they picked was Judge Kenesaw Mountain Landis. Landis took the game of baseball very seriously. He once said, "Baseball is something more than a game to an American boy. It is his training field for life work."

Landis didn't care that the eight White Sox players had been found not guilty. As the players celebrated, Landis released a statement to the press. It said, in part, "Regardless of the verdict of the juries, no player who throws a ball game, no player who sits in confidence with a bunch of crooked players and does not promptly tell his club about it, will ever play professional baseball."

BANNED FOR LIFE

The eight White Sox players were about to find out that Judge Landis meant exactly what he said. There would be no exceptions. Third baseman "Buck" Weaver found that out the hard way. From the beginning of the grand jury investigation through the trial, Weaver proclaimed his innocence. He admitted that he had been at a meeting or two when the fix was planned. But once he was on the field, Weaver had played his best. Everyone on the White Sox said so.

Judge Landis's parents named him Kenesaw Mountain because that was where his father served as a Union surgeon during the Civil War (1861–1865). While operating there, Landis's father narrowly escaped being killed by a cannonball.

37

★ ★ ★ ★

But Landis said that Weaver should have told the proper authorities about the fix and would not let him play. Weaver spent the rest of his life trying to get reinstated to play in the major leagues. When he became too old to play, he tried to become a coach or manager. But the answer was always the same: No.

Other White Sox players involved in the fix accepted Judge Landis's decision without a fight. Most of them played **semiprofessional** baseball for a while, then took ordinary jobs. Eddie Cicotte became a farmer and a **game warden**. Chick Gandil became a plumber. "Lefty" Williams ran a poolroom, then moved to California, where he managed a garden-nursery company. "Swede" Risberg became a dairy farmer, then ran a tavern. "Happy" Felsch also ran a tavern. Although **distraught** by the scandal, manager "Kid" Gleason managed the White Sox for three more seasons, and later was a coach with the Philadelphia Athletics for seven years until his death of a heart attack at the age of sixty-six.

A year after he was banned, "Shoeless" Joe Jackson—the most famous player of them all—appeared in a semiprofessional game in Hackensack, New Jersey. After whacking a double, a single, and a home run, someone finally figured out who he was. The losing team insisted that the game be declared a **forfeit**. Eventually, Jackson moved back to South Carolina and opened a dry-cleaning business. In 1924, he sued Charles Comiskey for back pay, and lost. Around that time, Jackson began to proclaim his innocence in the scandal. In his defense, Jackson's statistics in the 1919 World Series were incredible. His batting average was

JOB CHANGE

In September 1921, Arnold Rothstein announced he was through with gambling. Instead, he turned to **bootlegging** and drug dealing. In 1928, he was shot to death by a gambler named George McManus.

As time passed, other great players came on the scene and restored the public's faith in baseball. One, Babe Ruth, said he copied "Shoeless" Joe Jackson's hitting style because Jackson was the greatest hitter he had ever seen.

.375 and he got twelve hits, a record at the time. Many fans found it hard to believe that he wasn't trying to win.

Jackson spent the final years of his life running a liquor store. In 1951, there was a movement to clear his name. He was invited to New York to appear on a TV show celebrating his career. Jackson, however, died weeks before the trip.

Scandal still plagues major league baseball. Retired player Jose Canseco admitted to using steroids and accused other players of doing the same.

THE MODERN-DAY GAME

As time passed, most baseball fans forgave the White Sox players for their role in the baseball scandal of 1919. The public knew that what the players did was wrong. But some saw the players as victims of a system that allowed star players to be underpaid in an era when gamblers went unpunished.

Today, most modern ballplayers receive generous salaries. As a result, gambling isn't nearly as big a problem as it was in the early days of the game. But baseball is hardly problem-free. In the past several years, players have been accused of using illegal drugs called steroids. These drugs allow players to build up their muscles very quickly and hit the ball harder and farther. As a result, Major League Baseball has agreed to a stricter policy to keep players from taking steroids.

In the end, the story of the White Sox—whose former nickname, "The Black Sox," resurfaced because of the World Series scandal—should become a lesson to modern-day players. It is up to each generation of players to do all they can to keep the sport honest.

Despite the tremendous effect that the scandal of 1919 had on the sports world, the White Sox have managed to regain their reputation. The team celebrated a victory over the Houston Astros at the 2005 World Series.

Glossary

bootlegging—making and selling alcohol illegally

bribes—money paid to a person to convince him or her to do something illegal

distraught—filled with great emotional pain or sadness

evidence—the facts used to prove someone is guilty of a crime

forfeit—a loss because of an error, offense, or crime

game warden—person who enforces laws that protect wildlife from illegal hunting

gangster—a member of a gang of criminals

grand jury—a group of citizens brought together to investigate a possible miscarriage of justice

indicted—to be charged with a criminal offense

pennant—the team considered the winner of a league at the end of the season

reinstated—to be allowed to do something again

semiprofessional—an activity engaged in for pay, but not as a full-time job

stingy—not sharing one's resources with others

strategist—a person who is skilled at planning how to win a game or reach a goal

telegraph—a device for sending messages over long distances. It used a code of electrical signals sent by wire or radio, and was invented by Samuel Morse in 1837.

Timeline: The Black

1869

Professional baseball begins with the founding of the Cincinnati Red Stockings.

1876

The National League is formed.

1901

Charles Comiskey buys the Chicago White Stockings and their name becomes the White Sox.

1910

Comiskey opens Comiskey Park in Chicago.

1917

The Chicago White Sox win the World Series.

1919

SEPTEMBER 10
Chick Gandil tells gambler Joseph "Sport" Sullivan that the White Sox will throw the World Series for $80,000.

SEPTEMBER 21
Eight White Sox players meet in Gandil's room to discuss how they will throw the Series.

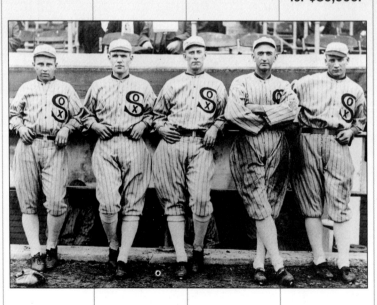

Sox Scandal of 1919

1920   **1921**

OCTOBER 1
Eddie Cicotte loses Game 1 of the World Series; the score is 9 to 1.

OCTOBER 8
Sullivan supposedly orders a gangster to talk to pitcher Williams.

OCTOBER 9
Williams loses the eighth game by a score of 10 to 5; Cincinnati wins the World Series.

OCTOBER 10
"Shoeless" Joe Jackson tries to tell Comiskey what happened; Comiskey refuses to see him.

AUGUST
A grand jury investigates gambling in baseball, including the 1919 World Series.

OCTOBER 2
Claude "Lefty" Williams loses Game 2 by a score of 4 to 2; catcher Ray Schalk is so suspicious that he attacks Williams after the game.

SEPTEMBER
Four White Sox players confess; gambler Arnold Rothstein says he is innocent.

The White Sox players are tried for conspiring to defraud the public and hurt the business of Charles Comiskey.

To Find Out More

BOOKS

Asinof, Eliot. *Eight Men Out*. New York: Henry Holt and Company, 1963.

Kinsella, W. P. *Shoeless Joe*. New York: Houghton Mifflin, 1982.

Ward, Geoffrey C., and Ken Burns. *Baseball: An Illustrated History*. New York: Knopf, 1994.

ONLINE SITES

1919 Black Sox.Com: The Story of the 1919 World Series Scandal

http://www.1919blacksox.com

1919 Black Sox Scandal

http://www.mc.cc.md.us/Departments/hpolscrv/blacksox.htm

1919 World Series: Black Sox Scandal

http://www.chicagohs.org/history/blacksox.html

Index

Bold numbers indicate illustrations.

About the Author

Dan Elish is the author of numerous books for children, including *The Worldwide Dessert Contest* and *Born Too Short: The Confessions of an Eighth-Grade Basket Case*, which was picked as a 2003 book for the Teen Age by the New York Public Library. He lives in New York City with his wife and daughter.